DISCARD

IGUANAS

THE REPTILE DISCOVERY LIBRARY

Louise Martin

WEST SLOPE COMMUNITY LIBRARY
3 78th AVE.
PORTLAND, OREGON 97225
DISCARD

Rourke Enterprises, Inc.
Vero Beach, Florida 32964

© 1989 Rourke Enterprises, Inc.

All rights reserved. No part of this book
may be reproduced or utilized in any form
or by any means, electronic or mechanical
including photocopying, recording or by any
information storage and retrieval system
without permission in writing from the
publisher.

Library of Congress Cataloging-in-Publication Data

Martin, Louise, 1955-
 Iguanas.

 (The Reptile discovery library)
 Includes index.
 Summary: An introduction to the iguana family,
their characteristics, behavior, and usefulness
to humans.
  1. Iguanidae—Juvenile literature. [1. Iguana]
I. Title.
II. Series: Martin, Louise, 1955-
Reptile discovery library.
QL666.L255M37   1989   597.95   88-30677
ISBN 0-86592-575-5

TABLE OF CONTENTS

Iguanas   5
How They Look   6
Where They Live   9
What They Eat   11
Horned Lizards   14
Marine Iguanas   16
Their Defenses   19
Baby Iguanas   20
Iguanas and People   22
Glossary   23
Index   24

IGUANAS

Members of the Iguanidae family are called iguanas. Iguanas exist in many different colors and sizes. In all, there are about seven hundred **species** of iguanas. Forty species can be found in the United States. One kind, the Florida scrub lizard, cannot be seen anywhere else. Most iguanas are between eight and fifteen inches long, although some can grow as long as six feet.

This land iguana lives in the Galapagos Islands

HOW THEY LOOK

Iguanas have scaly bodies and very long tails. An iguana's tail is usually twice the length of its body and head. Some iguanas have a crest, or ridge, running along their back and tail. Iguanas can move quickly on their long legs. Each toe has a strong claw that can be used for climbing. Male iguanas are normally larger than females.

Iguanas have bony crests and very long tails

WHERE THEY LIVE

Iguanas can be seen throughout North, South, and Central America. They also live on islands in the Caribbean and in the Galapagos Islands near Ecuador. Some species stay on the ground, while others live in trees. Iguanas can be found in woods and forests, close to rivers and streams. Iguanas often drop from trees into water if they are threatened. They are good swimmers and can escape their enemies easily that way.

Many iguanas live in trees

WHAT THEY EAT

Most iguanas are **vegetarian**. They live on berries, fruits, and young, tender leaves. Some iguanas also eat insects. Their diet may change during their lifetimes. While they are young, common, or green, iguanas *(Iguana iguana)* eat insects. As adults they feed mostly on the **vegetation** they find in their tree homes. They have also been known to eat birds and small **mammals**.

WEST SLOPE COMMUNITY LIBRARY
3670 SOUTHWEST 78th AVE.
PORTLAND, OREGON 97225

A land iguana feeds on a piece of cactus

Green iguanas like this are often kept as pets

Iguanas sometimes fight each other

HORNED LIZARDS

North America's most spectacular iguana is the horned lizard *(Phrynosoma cornutum)*. It is sometimes called the horned toad because its squat body is like that of a toad. Horned lizards have ten to twelve sharp spines on their bodies. These are very good defenses against snakes in the deserts where they live. Sometimes, if they are frightened, horned lizards cry small tears of blood.

A horned lizard peeps over a rock

MARINE IGUANAS

The marine iguanas *(Amblyrhynchus cristatus)* of the Galapagos Islands can grow to five feet long. They live in large herds on the rocky shores of the islands. To keep warm when swimming in the cold ocean, marine iguanas slow their heart beat. The blood then moves more slowly, taking longer to cool the iguanas' insides.

Marine iguanas live in the Galapagos Islands

THEIR DEFENSES

Iguanas are fiercely **territorial** creatures. They fight other iguanas that try to make a home too close to them. Some have colored throat fans that they show to their enemies to frighten them. Green iguanas have sharp, **serrated**-edged scales on their tails. When they whip their tails, the scales cut into the victim's flesh. Iguanas can even frighten off small dogs in this way.

This common iguana is showing its throat fan

BABY IGUANAS

Most iguanas lay eggs. The females dig a hole in the ground with their snouts or with their front legs. They lay the eggs in the hole and cover them over with loose earth. Female iguanas do not wait for the eggs to hatch. They take no further interest in their young. Some iguanas that live in cool places do not lay eggs. They bear live young instead.

Green iguanas hatch from eggs

IGUANAS AND PEOPLE

People sometimes hunt iguanas. South American Indians like to eat green iguanas and their eggs. They find the white flesh of green iguanas tender and very tasty. It is said to be similar to frogs' legs and is a great delicacy. A large, six foot long green iguana has a body length of two feet and can provide enough meat for a good meal.

GLOSSARY

mammals (MAM uls) — animals that give birth to live young and feed them with mother's milk

serrated (SAIR ay ted) — notched, like the edge of a saw

species (SPEE seez) — a scientific term meaning kind or type

territorial (tear uh TOR ee ul) — living in one area and not allowing other animals to enter

vegetarian (vej a TEAR ian) — an animal that only eats plants

vegetation (vej a TAY shun) — plant life

INDEX

Babies 20
Bodies 6, 14, 22
Color 5, 19
Crest 6
Defenses 14, 19
Diet 11
Eggs 20, 22
Enemies 9, 19
Legs 6, 20
Size 5, 16
Spines 14
Swimming 9, 16
Tails 6, 19
Throat fans 19